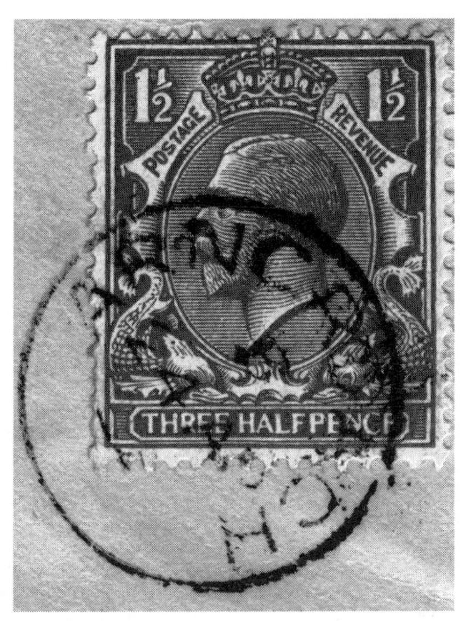

Old Kingsbarns, Largoward and landward villages of East Neuk

Eric Eunson

A reminder of the time when every village had its own post office and date stamp, before the advent of Mechanised Letter Offices and the blandly impersonal Edinburgh, Lothians, Borders and Fife cancellation which adorns Fife letters today. The post office at Stravithie was located in the railway station and operated from 1896 until closure in 1936. The other offices are described later.

First published in the United Kingdom, 2007,
by Stenlake Publishing Ltd.
www.stenlake.co.uk
ISBN 9781840334135

Laurel Bank and Ash Grove, a pair of handsome villas on the Cupar Road, Largoward in 1908. Much of Largoward is built from locally quarried whinstone, a hard volcanic rock measuring around seven on Moh's scale of mineral hardness, on which diamond is the hardest at ten! Although widely found in Fife it wasn't until the very end of the eighteenth century that this super durable material could be worked for building.

INTRODUCTION

In compiling these books of photographs from my collection of images of east Fife, it has been my custom to write a thumbnail history of the towns or villages featured, by way of an introduction. This latest compilation defies all attempts do to do this sensibly, covering, as it does, a substantial physical area and small villages and hamlets of diverse origin and function. Living in Colinsburgh for several years, I became acquainted with the landward portion of the East Neuk, and was frustrated that general histories mentioned these places almost not at all, and then often only the role some country laird had played in the great affairs of state.

These villages are largely overlooked by historians, tempted as they are by the rich heritage of the East Neuk, or overwhelmed by the antiquity of St. Andrews. En route to St. Andrews on the A915, visitors and local day trippers alike will fly through Largoward, unaware that they follow the feet of pilgrims along one of the oldest roads in Fife, or they will follow helpful brown signs along the A917 coast road, which tell them they are on the coastal tourist route.

There is another A class road betwixt the two, although it must have taken a vividly imaginative optimist with a sense of humour to have arrived at the classification; the A921 which diverges from the coastal route at Balchrystie, passes through Colinsburgh and, after the best motorcycling straight in the county, becomes a country back road from Newton of Balcormo by Arncroach and rejoins the coast road south of Kingsbarns. More frequented by tractors than tourists, it offers a glimpse of some of the best landscapes in rural Fife, and panoramic views to the coast. Along the way Kellie Castle and Scotland's Secret Bunker at Airdrie House, the East Neuk's worst kept secret even when it was an early warning station, might tempt a detour, but the beauties of Arncroach and Carnbee are not to be found in the standard guide books.

Beyond Crail the East Neuk ends with the official East Neuk of Fife at Fife Ness. Kingsbarns is left out, although motorists wing the village en route to the gardens at Cambo, and a new golf course *par excellence* has put Kingsbarns on the tourist map. Boarhills and Dunino, each with its simple kirk, are bypassed and ignored in favour of the Auld Grey Toun with its venerable university, cathedral and the Old Course.

The catchment area I have chosen is based on parish boundaries for the most part, viz. Kingsbarns, Cameron, Carnbee and Dunino, although Boarhills is included and lies near the margin of St. Andrews, and Largoward is just inside the edge of Kilconquhar, although it has little historical association with the southern part of the parish.
This little volume seeks in some small way to redress the balance a little, a book about the places other books ignore, the historical underdogs, which I hope will spark in locals and visitors alike an interest in some of the most appealing wee places in Fife.

This pretty corner in the grounds at Kellie Castle was photographed by William Easton of St. Monans in 1904.

Largoward has changed only a little since this view from the west was taken in 1909, but the skyline is no longer dominated by the colliery and its bing. The upgrading of the road from St. Andrews to Largoward into a turnpike was authorised in 1807, with tollhouses erected at Lathones and Higham before 1816. It was further extended to Upper Largo in 1829. Part of this was an ancient pilgrims' road dating back to the twelfth century or earlier. Pilgrims to St. Andrews crossed the Forth from North Berwick to Earlsferry and thence via Rires near Colinsburgh, to Gilston where the route joined the present road.

The dormers and porch had recently been added to the Staghead Inn when this 1909 postcard was published. The inn is thought to be contemporary with the extension of the turnpike road circa 1830, which formerly passed to the north of the building and not the south as it does now.

Largoward Town Hall was opened in 1907 and designed in a plain Art Nouveau style by A.S. Macrae. This view shows the location of the Largoward No.1 pit, about which little information can be traced, except that it came into being after the 1895 O.S. map was prepared and closed before 1914. Largoward underwent a period of growth in the 1830s, undoubtedly linked to an increase in coal mining in this period which would have benefited from recent road improvements. The East Fife Central Junction near Windygates had a station at Largoward. It ran to the south of the village and carried coal for shipment from Methil Docks. This goods railway operated from 1898 to 1964.

The Largoward coalfield was worked extensively here and in neighbouring parishes as far back as the reign of James VI (1567-1625), when an account once in the papers of Largo House described the delivery of coals from Falfield to Falkland Palace. It was extensively worked at Lathallan and several places on the Balcarres estate in the eighteenth century. In 1792 it was reported James Calderwood Durham of Largo House had a mine two miles in length at Largoward, which employed 37 men, with two grieves and an "oversman". This rare photograph shows Largoward No.1 pit. The Cassingray Colliery lay south of the village. Cassingray Colliery was operated by the Largoward Coal Company from 1900-05. At its peak in 1901 it employed 63 men below ground and 13 surfacemen.

Another view of Largoward No. 1 in 1905. The Baldastard Colliery worked the same coalfield on the northern edge of Largo parish from 1898-1902. The Largobeath Colliery was worked to the south east of the Largoward from 1910-1914, and at its peak in 1912 employed 110 men, more than the local area could provide. Extra miners were brought from Levenmouth and for a period the goods railway carried the only human traffic in its histtory. A further attempt to mine the Largoward coal at Falfield in 1937 was soon abandoned.

Largoward kirk still looks exactly as it did a century ago when this postcard was published. It was built as a chapel of ease in 1835, that is a place of worship within easy reach of population remote to the parish church at Kilconquhar. It was also used by people from New Gilston in Largo parish and by those living in portions of Cameron remote from their own parish church.

The school at Largoward is contemporary with the church, and in 1837 it is noted the heritors of Kilconquhar parish had set aside 100 merks for the salary of the schoolmaster there. The substantial schoolhouse was demolished in the 1970s.

A1909 postcard entitled "Awaiting Breakfast, R.H. Camp, Largoward". The Royal Highland Territorials were camped near the village in July 1909, and a huge photograph of the officers and men adorned the wall of the bar in the Staghead Inn until circa 2000 although its whereabouts is now unknown. The sender of the card comments to a friend in Braco, "Looks alright doesn't it? We have a large camp this year. Some great sport, very few tarts coming about but we have plenty football".

In 1910 it was the turn of the 8th Argyll and Sutherland Highlanders to hold their annual summer camp at Largoward.

Although Lathones is virtually conjoined to Largoward the villages lie in different parishes, Largoward being part of Kilconquhar and Lathones of Cameron. Lathones Church was opened as a Free Church after the Disruption of 1844. It was converted into a private house in the 1970s and is now minus its belfry. A post office opened at Lathones in 1855 but was replaced by a new office in Largoward in 1868.

The cottages on the left of this 1904 view of Lathones were completely ruinous until 2006 when a commodious modem house was erected on the site. The Lathones Hotel has been extended but this unusual picture remains otherwise much the same. The inn is contemporary with the turnpike road of circa 1830. A brief resumption of working the Largoward coalfield was attempted at Lathones in 1926 but was given up before 1939.

As far as I am aware this is the one and only picture postcard ever made of Radernie, which dates from 1905. In 1837 the working of limestone is described at Radernie and Winthank, the former being described as superior quality. It was wrought around thirty feet underground by boring the rock and blasting it with powder. The previous winter a waggonway had been constructed for the movement of the stone, and whinstone was also worked which was mainly used for road maintenance. Good coal was being wrought at this time at nearby Drumcarro. The last working of the Largoward coals was the Radernie Mine, which opened in 1930 and closed in 1946. The colliery consisted of two parallel drift mines and employed from 38-50 men.

Peat Inn, seen here around 1905, was previously known as Westfield of Radernie, although the Peat Inn name had come into use by the time the post office on the left of the picture was opened in 1855. Coal was worked extensively in this vicinity from the eighteenth century. At nearby North Falfield J.C. Durham of Largo House had erected a steam engine in 1784 to drain his mine, with a second in place by 1793. The Falfield pit employed some 40-50 men at this time with two grieves and an oversman. The coal from here was at least partly used to continue fuelling Durham's salt pans at Largo where local supplies had become exhausted. It was also reported he had "lately erected a number of colliers' houses". These were presumably the row at the entrance to Peat Inn which were restored from dereliction in the 1980s. Mining also took place at the Drumhead Pit immediately to the north east of Peat Inn, which was abandoned in 1300.

The smithy at Northtown of Falfield by Peat Inn on a postcard sent to Leven on Christmas Day 1905 by J. Wilson (right) who comments "Mother says I look like a beggar of course I am not dressed". The scattering of roadside blacksmiths' shops in this vicinity owe more to the needs of the long forgotten pits than agriculture. The Northtown forge is probably contemporary with a resumption of mining at Falfield by General Durham of Largo in 1831.

A binder is among the implements awaiting attention at the smithy in this 1920s view of Arncroach. Arncroach takes its name from *ard* and *cruach*, meaning the height of the stack, a reference to the 182 metre Kellie Law which overlooks the village. A large cairn on its summit is of unknown date and function, but is thought to be ancient.

Castle Street recalls the days before this 1920s picture was taken when this was a through road to Kellie Castle. Arncroach is the main village in the parish of Carnbee, but is not mentioned in any book before about 1840 and may have been primarily a new village of colliers. In 1793 it was reported that coal had formerly been worked in the parish at Over Carnbee, Balcormo (Newton) and Cassingray, although no coal was being wrought in the parish at that time.

Another view of Castle Street taken around 1908. Butler's House on the left is dated 1749 and is the oldest in the village and has been stripped of its render and restored. By 1844 two collieries had opened in the vicinity, one at Cassingray where coal had been worked before 1792 and another at Kellie. The Cassingray pit employed 38 colliers besides 3 labourers and two engine men; that at Kellie from 15-20 men, which together would account for a fair percentage of the population of Arncroach.

In 1844 it was reported a Free Church meeting house was being erected at Arncroach, which is shown on the right of this early 1930s picture. The school building behind is contemporary with the church, which closed in 1929 when the Free Church rejoined the Church of Scotland and the congregation merged with that of Carnbee, although there was some resistance from the Arncroach congregation. The schoolmaster's house on the left was demolished in the 1970s.

The house on the right of this view circa 1925 was enlarged in 1903 by Sir Robert Lorimer for Mr. Wheeler, his blacksmith. It was reported the wrought iron business had recently been discontinued in 1951, but the family were still engaged in making fine quality furniture. Arncroach had three shops in 1951, but only the sub post office now remains as the last shop in Carnbee parish. Arncroach post office opened on 2 September 1854.

Eighty years have seen a proliferation of dormers but Newton of Balcormo has otherwise changed little since this picture was taken. The name is an ancient one and means Cormack's town. The "Newton" suggests a connection with the Balcormo in Largo parish, but there is no confirmation of this.

Kellie Castle is an immaculately preserved monument in the care of the National Trust for Scotland. The north tower on the right of this 1909 view is the oldest part, dating from late fifteenth century, with fourteenth century origins. On the left is the south tower dating from 1603-6 which is contemporary with the block linking the two. The castle was abandoned and near derelict when it was acquired by Professor James Lorimer in 1878 who carried out a major restoration, continued by his son Sir Robert Lorimer (1864-1929). The relatively immature garden in the picture was Robert's work.

In June 1911 Robert Lorimer threw open the grounds of Kellie Castle for a sports day in honour of the coronation of King George V. This cock fight, photographed by William Easton of St. Monans, did not involve any feathered combatants, but rather two men with their arms tied to poles.

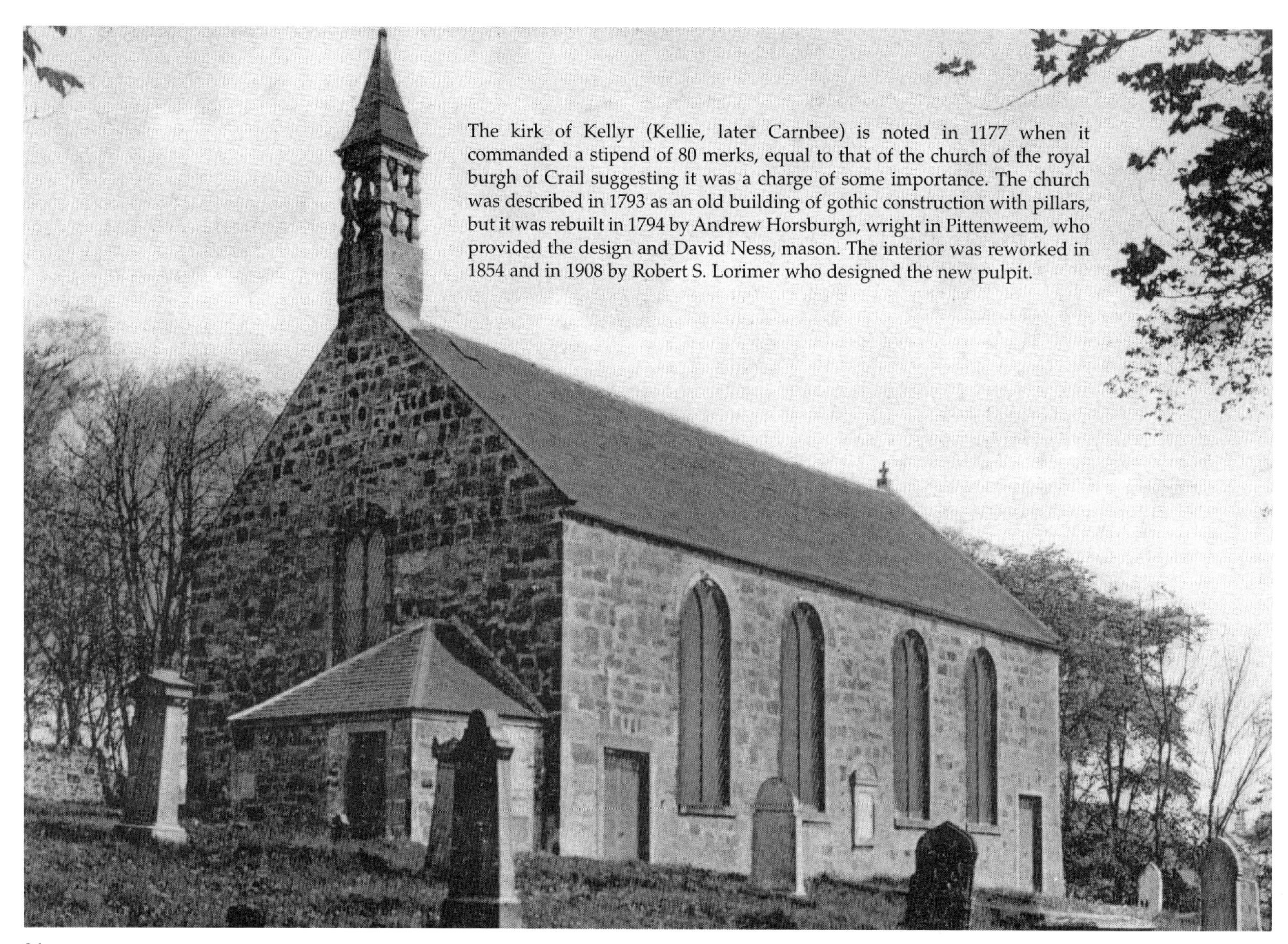

The kirk of Kellyr (Kellie, later Carnbee) is noted in 1177 when it commanded a stipend of 80 merks, equal to that of the church of the royal burgh of Crail suggesting it was a charge of some importance. The church was described in 1793 as an old building of gothic construction with pillars, but it was rebuilt in 1794 by Andrew Horsburgh, wright in Pittenweem, who provided the design and David Ness, mason. The interior was reworked in 1854 and in 1908 by Robert S. Lorimer who designed the new pulpit.

Carnbee

Carnbee Manse was built in 1819-20 by Thomas Clark and William Lees. It may have been designed by the surveyor George Dishington, who inspected the work. Carnbee is said to derive its name from *carn* and *bray* meaning birch hill. In 1752 the parish had a population of 1,293, which had fallen to 1,041 by 1793, a circumstance accounted for by the increased size of farms brought about by agricultural improvements. The parish was then let among 32 farmers, whereas there had been five times this number in 1700.

These cottages at Carnbee look exactly as they did a century ago. The population of Carnbee parish has fallen steadily since reaching a peak of 1,157 in 1861. By 1891 it had dropped to 952, by 1911 843, until by 1981 there were only 404 residents remaining.

Carnbee is first noted as having a school in 1642. In 1844 the parish contained one parochial school, one private and one female school. In addition to his salary the schoolmaster was provided with a house and also a portion of land at Over Carnbee which yielded an annual income of £20. The female school also came with a house and schoolroom together with the school fees. The teacher of the private school depended entirely on fees, which were inadequate for his support. The parish school then had a roll of 70. This view dates from circa 1930 and shows the war memorial on the right, which was unveiled ten years earlier.

Kingsbarns manse was erected in 1834-35, this photograph is about a hundred years later. The Pleasance was formerly known as Station Road. The village is said to derive its name from royal granaries located here from an early date; some sources suggest the reign of David I (1124-53) who had a royal residence at Crail. The village is said to stand on the site of the barns themselves. The remains of a castle a quarter of a mile from the village and of which there is no reliable history, were cleared away in the eighteenth century.

Kingsbarns became a separate parish devolved from Crail in 1631 and the lower part of the church tower is contemporary with this. The church building was entirely rebuilt in 1811 to a design by Robert Balfour. The top part of the tower and spire date from 1866. The bus in this view belonged to the Wemyss and District Tramway Company which was taken over by Alexander's in 1929 and this dates the view.

The Cambo Arms dates from the first quarter of the nineteenth century and has extensive stables to the rear. It was lately the subject of a successful campaign by locals to prevent its closure to be turned into housing, in 1755 the parish contained 871 inhabitants, and by 1792 this had fallen to 807. After reaching a peak of 937 the decline was steady, falling to just 638 by 1911 and 445 by 1981. In 1792 it was remarked there were 20-30 engaged in handloom weaving, who also worked at the fishing in season. Seafaring was preferred to the military life and there was seldom a season when some young men did not go to the Greenland whale fishing, which was still true in 1836.

The old pump in the Square is dated 1831. This was where the village's two annual fairs were formerly held in July and October, and the latter of these was where locals formerly stocked up with fresh meat for the winter months. Many drovers attended this fair with herds of black cattle, but by 1836 the fairs were much diminished and used only to display a few household items such as crockery. It seems Kingsbarns was considered an unhealthy place to live "the seat of agues and fevers and was certain to receive the visitations of every epidemic raging in the country".

In 1836 it was written of Kingsbarns "Within these ten years much has been done to remedy its unfortunate position. The streets have been properly levelled and metalled; many of the old and uncomfortable houses have been taken down; new ones with enlarged occupation within and neat flower pots in front erected; and from being one of the dirtiest and most unwholesome places of residence, it can now bear fair comparison to most of its neighbours". In the same year a peculiarity of the inhabitants was noted that they were often remarkable for height, and when the local militia were recruited more men in the grenadier company came from Kingsbarns than any other parish in eastern Fife. This view of the Seagate dates from 1921.

Kingsbarns post office opened in 1850 and was downgraded to a sub office of St. Andrews in 1930. It is still located in the third building from the left in this 1923 view, in 1951 it was remarked only three new houses had been built in the village in the preceding thirty years, and that most of the residents were elderly people.

The small yawl "Onward" photographed in Kingsbarns harbour in 1909. The harbour was built sometime after 1850 by a local farmer John Duncan to ship his potatoes to London. The south west pier was 220 feet long and the north west 410 feet, but it was abandoned and ruinous by the 1930s. Some years prior to 1792 large quantities of haddock had formerly been caught off Kingsbarns, but these had become rare although other species continued to be landed. Lobsters were also caught in the spring and summer but these were sent entirely to the London market. At this time there was a breakwater of sorts, but mooring posts were used to secure vessels as it was of no great strength.

This view of Kingsbarns golf course has to be one of the most boring postcards ever published, a definite off day for the photographer C.S. Burrows of Anstruther. The modest nine hole course was reported in the local press as reopening in 1923. Today it has been swamped by a vast state of the art course, reckoned to be one of the best in Fife.

A rare view of Kingsbarns railway station in the 1950s. The station was opened as part of the Anstruther and St. Andrews Railway on 1st September 1883, which included the stations at Crail, Kingsbarns, Boarhills, Stravithie and Mount Melville. The stations between Crail and St. Andrews were closed to passengers on 22 September 1930, and were finally closed to all traffic on 5 October 1964.

Stravithie House, by Dunino was erected in 1897 and was the home of Colonel Sprot, the Conservative candidate who unseated the former Liberal Prime Minister Herbert Asquith as M.P. for East Fife in 1918. The house was converted into flats in 1938. The site of an earlier castle of the same name lies to the north, probably the Strafatha referred to in a document of 1244. The moated castle with the remains of ornamental walks was still intact at the turn of the eighteenth century.

Dunino Church was erected in 1826-27 and designed by James Gillespie Graham. It has undergone some modifications since this 1905 view was taken and was remodelled by J. Jeffrey Waddell in 1928, who created a new entrance with a porch in place of the third window from the left and a chancel to the rear of the building. The manse was rebuilt in 1741 and 1819. Dunino was part of St. Andrews parish and is first noted as a parish in its own right in 1458. Some debate exists as whether the name is Dunino or Denino, the Dun prefix being normal until 1697, signifying a fortress. Other claim Denino describes its situation by a wooded den.

The simple interior of Dunino Church after its remodelling of 1928. The pulpit is by the celebrated architect Sir Robert S. Lorimer. The stained glass was executed by J. Jennings in 1930-31. This airy and bright little Arts and Crafts church is open for private contemplation and prayer throughout the year.

The Bel Craig is a man-made basin carved in an outcrop of rock not far from the church. Its age and purpose are unknown, and tales of druids collecting dew to sprinkle on devotees at Beltane may be taken as mere fantasy. In the den below are Celtic crosses engraved on the rock face but these seem to be hoaxes of comparatively modern date. A strange tale was recounted by a traveller in 1931 of a vision of a mysterious village at Dunino, inhabited by people in archaic dress, which on a later visit had vanished entirely. Curiously the Old Statistical Account of 1790 mentions some 60 years previously there had been around 30 houses in the village of which scarcely a trace then remained.

The ruined castle of Pittarthie stands in the midst of a field in the parish of Dunino, although it has been relieved of its foliage since this postcard was sent in 1920. It was built about 1580 for James Monypenny of Pitmilly, and was bought by William Bruce circa 1636. His son also William remodelled the house in 1682. It was bought by a Captain Cunningham circa 1760 and passed in time to his grandson Robert who was married to Susan Wise and had two children. In 1854 the whole family were wiped out in a shipwreck in Dublin Bay as they set out for a new life in Australia.

Boarhills lies close to the southern boundary of St. Andrews parish and has been almost entirely ignored by historians as in consequence. There was no church in the village in 1834 when an experienced Presbyterian probationer was appointed to act as preacher alternately at Boarhills, Strathkinness and Kincaple. Boarhills parish church was erected in 1866-67 and is described by one commentator as an "unlovable lanceted box", an uncharitable view of this simple kirk, enhanced by a commanding situation. This wintry view was sent in 1918.

The origin of the name Boarhills is subject to two explanations. When the relics of St. Andrew were supposedly presented to King Hungus of the Picts, who reigned from 731-761, he is said to have awarded the Culdees of the church of Kilrymont an area of land styled the Boar's Chase, which stretched from Largo to Naughton near Wormit and contained all the lands east of this line. Liddal in his "Place Names of Fife" offers a more prosaic explanation, that the name was formerly written as Byrhilis and means merely a place where there were byres for cattle.

The Main Street of Boarhills has changed little since this rare postcard was published some eighty years ago. The village was anciently known as Inch Murtach, the word Inch signifying in Gaelic not just an island but any good arable pasture ground. From the twelfth century until the time of the Reformation, the Bishops of St. Andrews had a palace on the foreshore at Inch Murtach, near the mouth of the Kenly Burn. All traces of it have now been erased apart from a doocot. Housing conditions in Boarhills are not described in 1951 but may be assumed to be similar to those in Dunino and Cameron parishes, where electricity had only reached the farms and larger houses, and internal hot and cold water and sanitation were sadly lacking.

The postie calls at the Boarhills store circa 1925. The sender of the card asks Miss Tulloch of Prestwick "Do you remember getting Pop a chocolate here? A bulldog lives here and I call on him each year".

A sub post office of Stravithie opened at Denino in 1856, and was renamed Dunino in 1930. This was the last shop in the parish when it closed in 1972. The post office at neighbouring Boarhills, seen here in 1925, was opened in 1851, and downgraded to a sub office of St. Andrews in 1917. This too has now closed.

Boarhills